The Supreme Court of India

1950-2000

The Supreme Court of India

Sentinel of Freedom

Published by the Supreme Court of India

EDITORIAL COMMITTEE: Hon'ble Justice B.N. Kirpal, Ashok H. Desai, Gopal Subramanium, Rajeev Dhavan, Raju Ramachandran

PROJECT CONSULTANT: Krishan Gabrani

TEXT: Rajeev Dhavan

PHOTOGRAPHY: Avinash Pasricha, Amit Pasricha

DESIGN: Shamli Nimbalkar

SPECIAL ACKNOWLEDGEMENTS: Dayan Krishnan, Nikhil Nayyar, Gaurav Kejriwal, Rajat Taimni, Siddharth Wahi, Shalinder Naryal

Printed at Ajanta Offset & Packagings Ltd.

ISBN 019565646-6

CONTENTS

FOREWORD

The Supreme Court of India was brought into being by the Constitution in 1950.

In the fifty years of its existence, the Supreme Court has witnessed India transit from colonial rule into a strong and independent secular democracy. Over these fifty years, both the political economy and the aspirations of India's uniquely diverse and, now, near one billion people have been transformed.

Concerned with the constitutional framework of the governance of independent India, the Supreme Court has watched over and participated in the affairs of the nation to try to secure an enduring foundation for a secular and democratic justice according to law for all. Not always without escaping criticism, the Court has constantly tried to respond to the problems, trials and tribulations of the people of India from whom the Constitution is derived and whose aspirations it seeks to serve. This Court has attempted to establish itself "in the consciousness of the people of India".

It is not easy to tell the story of the Supreme Court, which is imbricated in, and part of, the story of independent India. This little volume of pictures seeks to do no more than present a glimpse of the Supreme Court and its work over these tumultuous years.

A.S. Anand
Chief Justice of India

A view of the Judges' Library.

THE CONSTITUTION

AN ENDURING DOCUMENT

On the 26th day of November 1949, the people of India solemnly resolved to constitute a sovereign, democratic republic and give unto themselves a constitution. Titled the "Constitution of India" this document was to be the basis of governance for the generations to follow; and, to secure, Justice, Liberty, Equality and Fraternity "assuring the dignity of the individual and the unity of the Nation".

The Constitution established a federation of the Union and States, parliamentary institutions, a Bill of Rights in the form of a chapter on "Fundamental Rights", innovative "Directive Principles of State Policy" and a judiciary headed by the Supreme Court of India, with High Courts for every State, empowered to interpret and give effect to the Constitution and defend the rights and liberties of all persons and citizens.

The Indian Constitution, which the people had given unto themselves, was not just designed for a nation-State liberated from colonial rule, but for a veritable civilisation, which traversed an entire subcontinent across from the highest mountains in the world into the Indian Ocean. Within its domain lay a diversity of life, peoples, faiths and cultures that knows no parallel. Equally, India carried into the mid-20th century vast differences between the rich and the poor, the privileged and the disadvantaged, those with hope and those lost in despair.

The Constitution, and the institutions created by it, embodied the hopes of the people of India, of each and every citizen and of the shape of things yet to come.

The original Preamble read:

WE, THE PEOPLE OF INDIA, having solemnly resolved to constitute India into a
SOVEREIGN DEMOCRATIC REPUBLIC and to secure to all its citizens:
JUSTICE, social, economic and political;
LIBERTY of thought, expression, belief, faith and worship;
EQUALITY of status and of opportunity;
and to promote among them all
FRATERNITY assuring the dignity of the individual and the unity of the Nation;
IN OUR CONSTITUENT ASSEMBLY this twenty-sixth day of November, 1949, do HEREBY ADOPT, ENACT AND GIVE TO OURSELVES THIS CONSTITUTION.

It was for the people of India and the institutions of governance created by the Constitution to realise these expectations on an enduring basis for all times to come. One of these institutions of governance was the Supreme Court.

The Constitution, and the institutions created by it, embodied the hopes of the people of India.

THE INAUGURAL

"The Supreme Court will maintain the high traditions of the Judiciary and perform its duties without fear or favour".

On January 28, 1950, two days after India became a sovereign democratic republic, the Supreme Court had its inaugural session. The inauguration took place in the Chamber of Princes in the Parliament building, which also housed India's Parliament, consisting of the Council of States and the House of the People. It was here in this Chamber of Princes that the Federal Court of India had sat for 12 years between 1937 and 1950. This was to be the home of the Supreme Court for years until the Court acquired its own building.

The inaugural proceedings were simple but impressive. They began at 9:45 a.m. when the judges of the Federal Court – Chief Justice Harilal J. Kania and Justices Saiyid Fazl Ali, M. Patanjali Sastri, Mehr Chand Mahajan, Bijan Kumar Mukherjea and S.R. Das – "took their seats".

In attendance were the Chief Justices of the High Courts of Allahabad, Bombay, Madras, Orissa, Assam, Nagpur, Punjab, Saurashtra, Patiala and the East Punjab States Union, Mysore, Hyderabad, Madhya Bharat and Travancore-Cochin. Along with the Attorney General of India, M.C. Setalvad, were present the Advocates General of Bombay, Madras, Uttar Pradesh, Bihar, East Punjab, Orissa, Mysore, Hyderabad and Madhya Bharat. Present, too, were the Prime Minister, other Ministers, Ambassadors, Ministers and diplomatic representatives of foreign States, a large number of advocates of the Court and other distinguished guests.

Attorney General M.C. Setalvad extended "a cordial welcome (to) … the Supreme Tribunal of the Indian Union". Recalling the contribution of its immediate predecessor Federal Court, which "within its limited sphere … stood between the arbitrary action of the Executive and the people, endeavouring to safeguard the liberty of the subject", and that of the Privy Council whose judgements would, in his view, "continue to mould and influence the decisions of this Court", Setalvad reminded the Court that its writ

> "… will run over territory extending to two million square miles inhabited by a population of about 330 million … (to help build) a nation alive to its national and international duties, consisting of a strong Central authority and federated units each possessed of ample power for the diverse uses of a progressive people (and) … play a great and singular role and establish itself in the consciousness of the Indian people".

Chief Justice Harilal J. Kania responded by referring to the great constitutional changes that had occurred, complimenting the contribution of the Federal Court and Privy Council and whilst emphasising the limits within which the Supreme Court would discharge its duties he declared:

> "The Supreme Court, an all India Court, will stand firm and aloof from party politics and political theories. It is unconcerned with the changes in the government. The Court stands to administer the law for the time being in force, has goodwill and sympathy for all, but is allied to none. Occupying that position, we hope and trust, it will play a great part in the building up of the nation, and in stabilising the roots of civilisation which have twice been threatened and shaken up by two world wars, and maintain the fundamental principles of justice which are the emblem of God. We hope and trust the

Court will maintain the high traditions of the Judiciary and perform its duties without fear or favour. If we succeed in doing so we shall contribute our share to the progress of the Republic of India and render a service to the country which none else can render.... May God grant us the strength and wisdom to discharge the duties and functions of this Court".

Taking care to ensure that the Rules of the Supreme Court were published and the names of all the Advocates and Agents of the Federal Court were brought on the rolls of the Supreme Court, the inaugural proceedings were over and became part of the record of the Supreme Court.

The inaugural session of the Supreme Court of India on January 28, 1950, which took place in the Chamber of Princes of the Parliament House, was attended by a large gathering, including foreign guests. The photo shows a section of the invitees.

Hon'ble Sir Harilal J. Kania has the unique distinction of being the last Chief Justice of the Federal Court as well as the first Chief Justice of Supreme Court of India. He was the Chief Justice of India from August 14, 1947, until his death on November 6, 1951.

President Dr. Rajendra Prasad administers the oath of office to Sir Harilal J. Kania as the Chief Justice of India, as C. Rajagopalachari, the last Governor General of India, looks on.

The original Supreme Court. Sitting (from left) are: Hon'ble Mr. Mehr Chand Mahajan, Hon'ble Mr. Saiyid Fazl Ali, Hon'ble Sir Harilal J. Kania, Hon'ble Mr. M. Patanjali Sastri and Hon'ble Mr. B.K. Mukherjea. Standing (from left) are: N. Chandrasekhara Aiyar, S.R. Das and Vivian Bose.

THE COURT AND ITS PREDECESSORS

I

The Supreme Court established by the Constitution was empowered with a jurisdiction far greater than that of any comparable court anywhere in the world. It could virtually hear, decide and pronounce on any legal matter brought before it. As a *federal* court it had the exclusive jurisdiction to determine disputes between the Union of India and any State and the States inter se. As an *appellate* court, it could hear appeals from the State High Courts on civil, criminal and constitutional matters. It possessed a special appellate power to permit any appeals from any tribunal, court or High Court. In the years to follow, this latter special jurisdiction was to dwarf all others. It could review its judgements. In its advisory capacity, it could answer references by the President of India on any questions of law or fact, which had arisen or were likely to arise, that were of public importance.

The Supreme Court was empowered with a jurisdiction far greater than that of any comparable court anywhere in the world.

Its jurisdiction could be enlarged by Parliament. It could pass any decree and orders as was necessary for doing "complete justice". It had the power to punish for contempt of Court. The law declared by the Supreme Court was binding on all Courts within the territory of India. Interwoven into these powers was the power by judicial review – to strike down both legislation and executive action contrary to the provisions and the scheme of the Constitution, the distribution of power between Union and States, or inimical to the fundamental rights guaranteed by the Constitution.

The Constitution, with its guarantee of enforceable fundamental rights and an Indian Supreme Court, fulfilled a long-standing demand of India's independence movement. More than a hundred years ago, the Commonwealth of India Bill 1895, which the nationalist leader Annie Beasant described as the Home Rule Bill and which may have been "issued under Lokmanya Gangadhar Tilak's inspiration", proposed to reconstitute the Privy Council under a Lord Chancellor for India, puisne judges and Vice Chancellors. The proposed Privy Council was to discharge the judicial functions of Parliament. The President of Parliament was to be the head of the Privy Council in the absence of the Lord High Chancellor. Modelled as it was to reproduce the English system of governance on Indian soil, this scheme made no progress.

In the decades that followed, a clear view emerged that India's future Constitution should be drawn up under Indian inspiration. Following a "convention" in April 1924, a "Commonwealth of India Bill 1925" was drawn up to create a Supreme Court to determine federal and other questions and to be "the final appellate authority of India".

Around the same time the well-known lawyer, Sir Hari Singh Gaur, made five unsuccessful attempts in the Legislative Assembly to constitute an independent Supreme Court for India. It was only after the Round Table Conferences and the reports and White Papers that followed, that it became clear the future legislation envisaged a new court to decide constitutional issues.

The Government of India Act, 1935 created the Federal Court of India to interpret the Act of 1935, decide disputes between federating units and give its advisory opinions to the Government when asked to do so. Appeals from the Federal Court lay to the Privy Council in London, which remained the final arbiter on all the matters of the Indian legal system.

II

The Federal Court was in existence for only 12 years. But, it left behind a considerable impact on Indian law. The first Chief Justice of the Federal Court was Sir Maurice Gwyer. With him were appointed Sir Shah Sulaiman and M.R. Jayakar, who was replaced by Sir Srinivasa Varadachariar. When Sir Shah Sulaiman retired, Sir John Beaumont joined the Bench as an acting judge, and, later, Sir Muhammad Zafrulla Khan (who later emigrated to Pakistan).

If the principle of seniority of appointment had been followed, Sir Srinivasa Varadachariar would have succeeded Sir Maurice Gwyer on the latter's retirement on April 25, 1943. But, that

This rare photograph shows the inaugural sitting of the Federal Court of India on December 6, 1937. From left are: Hon'ble Mr. G. Davis, Hon'ble Sir J. Douglas Young, Hon'ble Sir Harold Derbyshire, Hon'ble Sir Shah Sulaiman, Hon'ble Sir Maurice Gwyer, Hon'ble Mr. M.R. Jayakar, Hon'ble Sir Courtney Terrel, Hon'ble Sir John Thom and Hon'ble Mr. J. Almond.

In 1950, when the Federal Court ceased to exist, its judges became judges of the Supreme Court, carrying with them a tradition of erudition, independence and courage.

was not to be. The British Government was not happy with some of his judgements. After a small gap, Sir Patrick Spens became the Chief Justice from June 8, 1943.

This is sometimes regarded as the first "supersession" controversy when the Government penalised a judge by not making him the Chief Justice of the highest court of the land because it did not like his judgements. As the judges retired or resigned, others were appointed in their place. Sir Torick Ameer Ali and Francis George Rowland were appointed acting judges of the Federal Court. In 1946, Sir Harilal J. Kania was appointed to the Federal Court, later to become its Chief Justice on August 14, 1947. He was joined in the Federal Court by Sir Saiyid Fazl Ali and M. Patanjali Sastri. After Independence, Mehr Chand Mahajan and Bijan Kumar Mukherjea were made judges of the Federal Court.

During the period of its existence, the Federal Court decided 151 cases, sitting at an average of 28 days a year! But, it decided issues of momentous importance relating to federalism, its own advisory jurisdiction and, more controversially, on matters of preventive detention (on which the dissenting view of Sir Srinivasa Varadachariar in 1943 may well have cost him the appointment as the permanent Chief Justice of the Federal Court).

In 1950, when the Federal Court ceased to exist, its judges became judges of the Supreme Court of India, carrying with them a tradition of erudition, independence and courage for its successor Court to follow.

III

In addition to the Federal Court, the new Supreme Court also replaced the Privy Council, which was the apex court of the system of law and justice administered by the British. Over the years, as British interest expanded from trade to empire, they experimented with various systems for the administration of justice. The East India Company had set up various courts of indifferent quality and questionable integrity in the territories occupied by them.

By 1726, "mayoral" courts emerged in the Presidency Courts of Bombay, Calcutta and Madras. After the battle for Bengal was won in the mid-18th century, the Company administered the Sadar Dewani and Sadar Nizamat Adalats from which appeals lay to the Privy Council. Different courts dealt with "foreigners" and "natives". The Supreme Court of Judicature of Calcutta was created for Bengal in 1773. The Recorders Courts created for Bombay and Madras in 1798 replaced the mayoral courts; and were themselves replaced by Supreme Courts in 1823.

Conflicting jurisdictions over "foreigners" and "natives" and between the Presidency towns and the other areas created great confusion. In 1829, a Chief Justice of the Supreme Court Calcutta lamented "the utter want of connection" between these two systems of justice that competed with each other and viewed each other with jealousy! Nor, as a despatch from London of 1834 made abundantly clear, did the British want "(a) judicature utterly uncontrollable by the government, and, on the contrary, controlling the government, recognising the highest authorities of the state as private individuals".

After the First War of Independence in 1857, the Indian High Courts Act of 1861 abolished the erstwhile Supreme Courts and Sadar Adalats – leaving it to Her Majesty to issue Letters Patents under the Great Seal of the United Kingdom for the creation of a High Court.

The Charter of the Calcutta High Court was issued on May 14, 1862, and published in Calcutta on July 1, 1862. The Charters of the Bombay and Madras High Courts, which were issued on June 26, 1862, were found to be defective and reissued on December 28, 1865. The Charter of what is now the Allahabad High Court was issued on March 17, 1866, for the High Court of the, then, North Western Provinces. First established in Agra, it was later shifted to Allahabad in 1875. The territory of Avadh had a Court of Judicial Commissioner from 1865 with its own territorial jurisdiction. It merged with the Allahabad High Court on July 26, 1948.

The Indian High Courts Act, 1861, and later the Government of India Act, 1915, also enabled the creation of the Patna High Court for the territories of Bihar and Orissa. The High Court of Lahore was chartered on March 21, 1919, and a Charter was issued to create the High Court of Nagpur for the Central Provinces on July 2, 1936.

With the High Courts, the earlier dual system of justice was integrated into one. In the latter part of the 19th century, large parts of "British" Indian law were reduced to statute. However, there remained vast areas of law – such as the personal and customary laws of the various communities – which remained uncodified and which were administered by the courts according to "justice, equity and good conscience".

Appeals from the High Courts lay to the Privy Council. In 1928, in a famous speech in the House of Commons, Lord Brougham expressed astonishment that the government and a trading company together ruled over not less than 70,000,000 subjects stretching from the Indian Ocean to the Pole, to exercise an immense jurisdiction over persons and property on legal and political matters on vast and varied questions through a Privy Council which was unaided and alone.

With the enactment of the Judicial Committee Act, 1834, the work of the Privy Council was placed on a much more systematic basis. It was a court of many colonial achievements, which – along with the High Courts in India – had laid the foundation for the application of English and other laws in India to an extent that continues to carry persuasion in our times. But, although distinguished Indians were made members of the Privy Council and contributed greatly to its endeavours, it was not an Indian court, by and for Indians. Years later, Mahatma Gandhi, commenting on the Privy Council, observed:

> "... on highly intricate matters of custom, in spite of all their labours, they have often made egregious blunders".

Despite its enviable contribution in interpreting Indian law in the light of English doctrine, the Privy Council remained an English court operating from Whitehall in London. Appeals to the Privy Council were abolished in 1949 just before the Constitution of India came into being. It was as inevitable as it was historically compelling that the Supreme Court had to be an Indian court established by Indians to participate in the future life and fortunes of the Indian nation.

APPOINTMENT OF JUDGES

I

The original Indian Constitution of 1950 envisaged a Supreme Court with a Chief Justice and seven puisne judges – leaving it to Parliament to increase this number. In the early years, all the judges of the Supreme Court sat together to hear the cases presented before them. As the work of the Court increased and arrears of cases began to accumulate, Parliament increased the number of judges from eight in 1950 to 12 in 1956, 14 in 1960, 18 in 1978 and 26 in 1986. As the numbers of the judges have increased, they have sat in smaller benches of twos and threes – coming together in larger benches of five and more only when required to do so, or to settle a difference of opinion or controversy.

The first Chief Justice of India was Sir Harilal J. Kania. He had been a judge of the High Court of Bombay and later the Chief Justice of the Federal Court. In 1950, he was joined by judges with varied experiences drawn from different parts of the country. Saiyid Fazl Ali had been called to the Bar in England, practised in and had been a judge of the Patna High Court before he became a judge of the Federal Court in June 1947. M. Patanjali Sastri came from the Madras Bar, and was a judge in the Madras High Court before his appointment to the Federal Court in December 1947. Mehr Chand Mahajan had been a lawyer and judge in Lahore (and, later – after Partition – in the High Court of East Punjab) before he became a judge of the Federal Court in October 1948.

Known for his robustness and varied interests, Mahajan devoted a very small part of his autobiography, *Looking Back* (1963), to his judicial experiences in the Supreme Court. Since appeals to the Privy Council were abolished, he also headed the Supreme Court bench with two *ad hoc* judges – Justices R.S. Naik and Khaliluzzaman to hear the pending cases in appeals from the State of Hyderabad.

Sudhi Ranjan Das had been called to the Bar in England, and had practised at Calcutta before becoming a judge of the Calcutta High Court and later Chief Justice of the East Punjab High Court. He was appointed to the Federal Court on January 20, 1950 – just a few days before the Supreme Court came into being.

All these judges – except Saiyid Fazl Ali – were destined to become Chief Justices of India in the decade that was to follow. Since there were still vacancies to the Supreme Court, N.C. Aiyar, a former lawyer, district judge and retired High Court judge from Madras, and Vivian Bose, a barrister who had practised in, and was Chief Justice of, the Nagpur High Court, were appointed to the Supreme Court in 1950.

These eight judges, who constituted the Supreme Court of India in the first year of its inception, brought together an incomparable collective talent of knowledge, pragmatism, sense of justice, sobriety and vision. Often disagreeing with each other, these judges steered the Supreme Court through the first and most difficult years of its history.

II

On November 6, 1951, Chief Justice Kania died. It was a terrible blow to a Court that in its first few months was confronted by many controversies. The immediate question was: Who was going to be the next Chief Justice of India? It is difficult to say what discussions took place behind the scene. In those days, much was left to trust and a common understanding evolved between the Union Government led by Jawaharlal Nehru and the judiciary.

Even before 1950, a tradition had developed that the senior-most judge of a High Court would become its Chief Justice unless there were special reasons for not doing so. Such a practice had been deviated from by the British – most significantly in not making Sir Srinivasa Vardachariar the Chief Justice of the Federal Court in 1943, and bringing in Sir Patrick Spens to supersede him.

It is said that at some stage in the early 1950s, Prime Minister Nehru may have contemplated bringing in a Chief Justice of India from outside, to pass over the claims of the sitting judges of the Supreme Court. Whether this was really the case – or even a serious proposal – is not entirely clear. But, the decision to appoint Justice Patanjali Sastri to succeed Chief Justice Harilal Kania was followed in the appointment of Justice Mehr Chand Mahajan to succeed Chief Justice Sastri and Justice B.K. Mukherjea to succeed Chief Justice Mahajan as Chief Justices of India. This practice has endured for all, but two appointments in 1973 and 1977, irrespective of the consequence that the Chief Justice so appointed would hold office for only a few days.

The first "supersession" took place soon after the judgement in the *Fundamental Rights* case (1973), which was decided on April 24, 1973. Chief Justice S.M. Sikri was due to retire soon after, on April 26. If the now established principle of seniority had been followed, J.M. Shelat would have become Chief Justice for a few months, K.S. Hegde for almost one year and A.N. Grover for two years and eight months. But, the Government of the day decided to appoint the fourth puisne judge, A.N. Ray, Chief Justice of India, who was never in the reckoning for such an appointment on the basis of the principle of seniority.

The reason for this "supersession" can be traced to the various judgements delivered in the *Fundamental Rights* case (1973). The majority of judges in the *Fundamental Rights* case (1973), which included the three superseded judges, took the view that Parliament could not indiscriminately amend the Constitution. Any amendment to the Constitution was subject to the implied limitation that the "basic structure" of the Constitution could not be amended.

The *Fundamental Rights* case (1973) had assembled together the largest-ever bench of 13 judges that the Supreme Court had ever known. It had laid down a new and impressive doctrine that other countries now cite with approval and, perforce, distinguish without disapproval. The "basic structure" doctrine has found its way into the Constitutions of some States. The "supersession" was directly linked to judgements in this and other cases.

Even before 1950, a tradition had developed that the senior-most judge of a High Court would become its Chief Justice unless there were special reasons for not doing so.

The Government of the day did not cloak its discomfiture. It openly declared that it had the power to appoint whomever it liked. Mohan Kumaramangalam, the Minister of Petroleum and Mines, openly defended the "supersession" by talking of the need for "committed" judges. This was openly stated in Parliament; and later published as a book on *Judicial Appointments.*

But, who were "committed" judges? The Government claimed that the "committed" judges were to be judged by their ideology and the socialistic and other needs of the nation. There were angry protests both over the "supersession" and the "committed judge" theory offered as a justification for it. There was a suspicion that the "commitment" that the Government was asking for was not to an ideology, but to the regime in power.

The "supersession" of 1973 was self-evidently punitive – seeking to punish those judges who had decided the *Fundamental Rights* case (1973) and other cases against the Government. Perhaps, the Government wanted to change the time-honoured principle of seniority and claim the power to appoint Chief Justices of its own choice and patronage.

All this was implicit in the theory of a "committed" judge. And, if the Chief Justice had to be a "committed" judge, the same yardstick would, perforce, apply to the initial appointment of puisne judges as well. The suspicion that potentially future Chief Justices of India could be punished for deciding against the Government gained ground – all the more so during the Emergency (1975-77), when several High Court judges, who took a stance against the Government, were punitively transferred without their consent to other High Courts.

The view that Supreme Court judges could be punished for not deciding cases according to the Government's liking became clear with the "second supersession" of 1977. During the Emergency, in the *Preventive Detention* case (1976) the Court divided by four votes to one, to virtually abandon its power of judicial review even in cases where detentions had been made in bad faith.

The majority consisted of Chief Justice A.N. Ray (the beneficiary of the "first supersession") and three judges (Justices M.H. Beg, P.N. Bhagwati and Y.V. Chandrachud), who would become Chief Justices of India at some later stage if the seniority principle were to be adhered to. The dissenting judge was Justice H.R. Khanna, who was to be the next Chief Justice of India after Chief Justice Ray retired on January 29, 1977. Unhappy with Justice Khanna's dissent, the Government superseded him and appointed Justice Beg as the Chief Justice.

After the Emergency (1975-77), the new Janata Government could well have declined to follow the seniority principle and penalised the majority judges in the *Prevention Detention* case. But, it did not do so. The principle of seniority has been followed since – to receive a measure of recognition in the judgements of the Supreme Court itself.

So far, there have been 29 Chief Justices of India.

III

Although the Constituent Assembly, which drafted India's Constitution, was somewhat wary about entrusting too much power with the judiciary, no detailed view was expressed on the kind of judges who should be appointed to the Supreme Court and High Courts. There was some discussion that those who had been ministers in the Union or in the State should be excluded from appointment to the Supreme Court. It was also the unanimous view of a conclave of judges that members of the Indian Civil Service should not be made the permanent Chief Justice of any High Court.

If all this had been carried, Justice Krishna Iyer, who had been a minister in the Kerala Government of 1957, would have been excluded from appointment. Many judges from the Indian Civil Service, who had chosen a judicial career, may not have been appointed Chief Justices of their Courts or, consequently, judges of the Supreme Court. The text of the Constitution imposed no disqualifying constraints of this nature; it laid down broad qualifications as to who was eligible for appointment as a judge of the Supreme Court of India. Perhaps, Prime Minister Nehru's passing comment expressed the mood of the Assembly when he said:

> "(A) man appointed to the Federal Court is presumably one who has gone through an apprenticeship in the High Court somewhere. He cannot be absolutely bad, otherwise he would not have got there. He must have distinguished himself in a High Court as Chief Justice or something".

Instead of indicating on the kind of judges to be appointed, the Constitution devised the procedure to be followed – into which it had built procedural safeguards.

Having indicated the three categories of persons who were eligible for appointment – that is to say High Court judges who had served in one or more Courts, lawyers who had been advocates of one or more High Courts and those who, in the opinion of the President of India, were distinguished jurists – the Constitution indicated the manner of appointment:

> "Every Judge of the Supreme Court shall be appointed by the President by warrant under his hand and seal after consultation with such of the Judges of the Supreme Court as the President may deem necessary for the purpose and shall hold office until he attains the age of sixty-five years".

It was through this consultative procedure that appointments were amicably made for many years.

The first few rumblings that this simple formula of consultation had failed came from various quarters after the "first supersession" in 1973. Former Chief Justices of India and judges of the

"Every Judge of the Supreme Court shall be appointed by the President ... after consultation with such of the Judges of the Supreme Court as the President may deem necessary for the purpose".

Over the years, judges have had a camaraderie which alone can make the Supreme Court viable as an institution of governance.

Supreme Court, leading lawyers and others expressed anguish over what had been done. Proposals were made to create a consultative collegiate which would recommend appointments to the President. This would have called for amendments to the Constitution. The proposal was not taken further, but the idea survived to surface in the form of suggestions from time to time.

By 1981, when Mrs. Indira Gandhi returned to power, the issue of judicial appointments re-surfaced. In the *Judges* case (1981), the nature of the consultative system envisaged by the Constitution was examined by the Supreme Court. If too much was read into the process of consultation, the consultees would virtually become the appointing authority. If too little was read into this process, the path was wide open for political appointments. Amidst a diversity of views, the judges accepted that consultation was crucial, but did not make the advice of the judges "binding" on the Government.

Intuitively, the judges seemed to have a residuary faith in the practices that had developed since Independence; and hoped that these would continue. In the *Second Judges* case (1993), these intuitions were reinforced by the Supreme Court laying down the necessity of consultation with the Chief Justice and his colleagues, elaborating the procedures to be followed and leaving the Government the option of disagreeing for good reasons in writing

In the *Third Judges* case (1998), the Court went further to emphasise that the Chief Justice was consulted as the representative of the judiciary and not in his personal capacity to virtually create a collegiate of, at least, the five senior-most judges and reinforce the procedure to be followed. One answer given to critics that the Court had gone overboard to invent a collegiate and lay down elaborate procedures was that the Supreme Court has done no more than consecrate the best practice that had prevailed over the past five decades, if not longer.

Over the past 50 years, 139 judges have been appointed to the Supreme Court. They have come from varied backgrounds, from different States and with different views on many matters — and enriched by their personalities. Yet, they have had a togetherness, which alone can make the Court viable as an institution of governance.

IV

Perhaps, the variety of judicial appointments and the convivial camaraderie that exists amongst the judges is best brought out in an interesting speech by Chief Justice S.R. Das when he demitted office in 1959:

"If I may now digress a little, I have noticed that each of my past colleagues had some technique of his own. I shall only refer to the technique of stopping irrelevant arguments. One was the logical approach. The exponent of this technique was Chief Justice Kania. When an advocate would go on and on and enunciated an untenable proposition of law, tilting his head on one side Chief Justice Kania would say, 'So what? What is the sequitur?' As there was really no sequitur, the argument had to stop. The other was, what we call, the humane approach and that was Fazl Ali's. He used to say, 'Your arguments are very attractive, I must say, and I have made a note of them.' Then followed a disarming smile, which effectively stopped the argument. The third was the direct approach and Chief Justice Mahajan was its exponent. I will tell you an interesting story. There was an appeal before us in a case where a man alleged that he had been wrongfully dismissed. It was a case of company in which there were two sets of directors and they were fighting and were at loggerheads. This man who was the manager had sided with one of the factions and when ultimately the other faction came into power, they promptly dismissed him. Counsel came from outside. He was going on arguing. There was nothing in the case. Then, Chief Justice Mahajan, who was presiding, looked at him frowningly and said, 'Why did you take sides?' Counsel replied, 'What could I do? They were the men in power'. Chief Justice Mahajan looked at him and said, 'So you believe in obeying the men in power?' He said, 'Yes, my Lord, what could I do?' Quick came the reply, 'I am the man in power here. You had better sit down'. And the counsel actually did what he was told!

"Before I finish, I should refer to my present colleagues. We have been, indeed, a very happy family. There is my successor-designate. He relieves us from the monotony of our Court work by quoting couplets from Urdu and Persian poets and our minds are immediately refreshed. Then we have brother Imam, all the time trying – but never succeeding – to convince the advocate that his arguments are entirely useless. Then comes my friend S.K. Das. He is there all the time cutting jokes and pulling our legs, using chaste language and very good at quotations, many of which are not fit for the Presidential ear. Then comes my brother Kapur. When an argument is in full swing, he distinctly remembers that there is a decision, either of the House of Lords or of the Privy Council, which is pat on the point under discussion; but, unfortunately, that decision he cannot, for the moment, lay his hands on, and all the members of the Bar appearing in the case cannot find it till the case is over. Then comes my learned brother Gajendragadkar. His heart is literally bleeding for the underdogs, and, unless the bleeding can be stopped, the underdogs will very soon become the top dogs. My brother Sarkar has been an onlooker on the highway of life. He attends dinners, but does not eat; he sees other people eat. He has joined many bridal processions, but has not married. But I do not know whether he will change his mind. Then we have brother Subba Rao who is extremely unhappy, because all our fundamental rights are going to the dogs on accounts of some ill-conceived judgements of his colleagues, which require reconsideration.

"There is brother Wanchoo. Sometimes when it is said that U.P. is not represented in his court we point our finger to brother Wanchoo; and when it is said that Rajasthan is not represented, there is brother Wanchoo. He has the best of both worlds. Then we have brother Hidayatullah. He has given us three gospels – Stroud's Judicial Dictionary, Wilson's Glossary, and Words and Phrases by some author whose name I forget. I do not know when he will produce the fourth Gospel.

"Last but not the least is my brother K.C. Das Gupta. He is a dark horse, and it is too early to appraise his merit."

Chief Justice Das could not have put it better.

There is very little written by or on judges. Not many inside stories or personal insights emerge in what is written.

Judges of the Supreme Court have been called upon to give judgements on issues of monumental judicial significance.

V

On a general overview to date, of the 139 judges (excluding Justices R.S. Naik and Khaliluzzman, who formed part of a Bench to hear appeals from Hyderabad) appointed to the Supreme Court, four were directly recruited to the Court from the Bar, eight were judges belonging to the Indian Civil Service and therefore never practised at the Bar; one retired from the I.C.S. in 1951 and joined the Bar, and five other judges had judicial training in subordinate courts.

Amongst the lawyer-judges recruited from the various High Courts, which numbered around 129, many had at some stage been Advocates General of their respective States. Of the four lawyers who were directly appointed to the Supreme Court, one was the Advocate General of Punjab, one had been Additional Solicitor General of India and one had been Additional Solicitor General and Solicitor General of India. Several others had worked as lawyers for their respective State Governments. The remaining judges had reasonably long careers as practising lawyers.

As regards judicial experience, six had been judges of the Federal Court of India, 62 Chief Justices of various High Courts and 75 puisne judges of the High Courts they were recruited from.

As regards their educational qualifications, 29 judges received some of their university education in England, and 25 were called to the Bar at one of the Inns of Court in London. This means that a total of 23 percent of the judges received university or professional education in England. The rest of the Court was educated in India; at least six were scholars of Sanskrit. Several judges did post-graduate research. B.K. Mukherjea was a Tagore Law Professor and delivered lectures on the Hindu law relating to Religious Endowments and J.M. Shelat wrote a post-graduate thesis on the United States Senate. A.S. Anand and T.K. Thommen completed doctorates in law.

While many judges of the Supreme Court have been associated with academics, very few of them have had political experience. B. Jagannadhadas had been imprisoned for the part he played in the freedom movement, J.L. Kapur had some trade union backing, G.L. Oza also participated in the freedom movement and had suffered detention in the 1930s, Patanjali Sastri had been a member of the Madras Legislative Council and K.S. Hegde had been a Member of Parliament. Bahrul Islam was elected Member of Rajya Sabha in 1962 and 1968. K. Subba Rao resigned as Chief Justice of India to unsuccessfully contest the election for President of India. V.R. Krishna Iyer had been a Cabinet Minister in Kerala and later a High Court judge. At the time of his appointment, Krishna Iyer was a member of the Law Commission.

Supreme Court judges are usually appointed between the ages of 51-1/2 and 62. The average age on appointment is 57 years. Four were appointed to the Supreme Court after they had retired as judges of their respective High Courts. The judges retire at the age 65.

Over the years, judges of the Supreme Court have been called upon to give judgements on hundreds of thousands of cases and issues, many of them of monumental constitutional and judicial significance.

INTERPRETING THE CONSTITUTION

I

The first case to be decided by the Supreme Court was *R.K.R. Agarwal of Kamptee v. Secy. Municipal Committee, Kamptee.* It was a civil matter that did not portend what lay in store for the Court.

The constitutional history of the Supreme Court began with the case, *A.K. Gopalan v. State of Madras* (1950). Using the provisions of the Constitution, which permitted direct recourse to the Supreme Court for the infringement of any person's fundamental rights, the Communist leader, A.K. Gopalan, protested that his preventive detention without trial was illegal, *mala fide* and unconstitutional. No reasons for the detention were disclosed to him. A statutory bar prevented such disclosure even though the Constitution required it. Most skilfully, Gopalan's lawyer, M.K. Nambyar, argued that India too had a due process clause like America, requiring statutes by Parliament to conform to universal standards of justice.

A.K. Gopalan both succeeded and failed in his endeavours. The Supreme Court used its powers to strike down the "non-disclosure" provisions. All the judges, except Saiyid Fazl Ali, refused to accept the broader due process argument – perhaps because they were aware that the Constitution makers had specifically thrown out any reference to due process from the text of the Constitution and replaced it with "any process" clause to permit infringement of fundamental rights made into "according to procedure established by law".

Gopalan's case tested the strength and resilience of the Supreme Court. The Court responded with an incisive courage. It revealed its full authority to strike down constitutionally wanting legislation. But it used this power only to strike down one section of the Act.

Declaring its undoubted power to be the final custodian to interpret the Constitution, the Supreme Court gave a modest interpretation, resisting wider notions of "due process" with which it was not immediately comfortable. The Government had no cause for complaint. Gopalan was not released from imprisonment. But, he could pursue other remedies to secure his release. That the Court proved to be wrong in its interpretation of the Constitution and due process in the decades that were to follow is another matter. Within weeks of its coming into existence, the Supreme Court had established its undoubted power of judicial review over all acts of the executive and legislation; and to be the final arbiter of the Constitution.

Gopalan was only a declaration and a glimpse of the Court's vast powers of judicial review and constitutional interpretation. In the *Cross Roads* and *Organizer* cases (1950), the Supreme Court was confronted with the issue of the pre-censorship of publications by the press. Recognising that "freedom of speech and the press lay at the foundation of all democratic organisation" and that "without free political discussion no public education, so essential for the proper functioning of the process of popular government, is possible", the Court gave a strict interpretation that the Constitution permitted restrictions on the grounds of "security of State" but not public order. In these circumstances the action of pre-censorship was unconstitutional. This judgement had the wider

Freedom of speech and the press lay at the foundation of all democratic organisation.

effect of curtailing the Government's powers to censor free speech even if there was a danger to public order.

But, there was more on the horizon. The Constituent Assembly had gone to some lengths to discuss and provide protection for pending agrarian reform legislation, which aimed to appropriate the property of traditional *zamindars,* landlords and others and redistribute it to the poor (1950-51). The High Courts of Bihar, Uttar Pradesh and several others struck down agrarian legislation that offered little or illusory compensation to the former landowners. Appeals were filed in the Supreme Court.

To add to this stream of controversial matters were the *Preferential Treatment* cases (1950) from Madras, where the Court struck down schemes that generally distributed a largesse of opportunities and benefits to castes and communities. This, as the Court said, was impermissible, while generally casting some doubt on the possibilities of affirmative action for the disadvantaged. The Government in power was astonished and annoyed by these judicial decisions. From its point of view, the Court had assumed a very broad power of judicial review, struck down the power to restrict speech that could lead to disorder, cast inchoate doubts about the possibilities of affirmative action for the truly disadvantaged and undermined the agrarian reform programme by supporting undeserving landlords. Prime Minister Nehru ruefully said:

> "Somehow we have found this magnificent constitution that we have framed was later kidnapped and purloined by the lawyers".

The struggle for judicial review was well under way.

The Government responded to these Court decisions by amending the Constitution. The relatively minor amendments were those that enabled restrictions on free speech in the interest of public order and removed possible obstacles in the path of affirmative action. The more major amendments were elaborate to protect agrarian reform legislation from excessive judicial scrutiny at the behest of landlords. These elaborate amendments paved the way for a continuous stream of future amendments, which would take away judicial review, ostensibly in the public interest.

The Supreme Court reacted to these amendments of 1951 in a variety of ways. In the *First Amendment* case (1951), it refused to accept that Parliament did not have the power to amend the Constitution – a view that would later be reviewed and reversed. In the *Land Reform* cases (1992), the Court struck down provisions of the Bihar legislation that gave little or insufficient compensation on the grounds that the legislature had indulged in a "colourable" exercise of power, which was a fraud on the Constitution. Such a concept of colourability had infinite possibilities and was read down by the Court itself in a later decision the next year.

In 1952, the Supreme Court changed the emphasis on its interpretation of the concept of the "security of State" and free speech. But, it held its ground on the manner in which acquisitions of property were being made with insufficient recompense. In a round of property cases in 1954, the Court was unequivocal that the guaranteed fundamental right to property in the Constitution required that full compensation be paid at market value to those whose property was taken away.

The Fourth Amendment to the Constitution in 1954 sought to reverse the decisions of the Supreme Court on the compensation payable and to give further immunity of protection to various legislations from judicial review by the Courts. Many other amendments followed. Some were routine in relation to the reorganisation of Indian federalism in 1956. Some, like the Seventeenth Amendment in 1962, were to protect agrarian reform legislation. For a little while these issues, which had brought the Supreme Court and the Government at loggerheads with each other, lay fallow – to erupt again in the mid-1960s.

II

Too angular a view cannot be taken of these tensions between the Government, Parliament and the judiciary. The Supreme Court had declared and established its undoubted power of judicial review and to interpret the Constitution. It had struck down provisions it found to be unwholesome. Faced with amendments, it had modified its stance. If an overall review is made of the Court's judgements for these first five years, it had – by and large – supported the elaborate regulatory framework, which the Government had imposed upon the economy.

Soon after his retirement, Chief Justice Patanjali Sastri told the Madras Lawyers Conference in 1955 that the Court had been misunderstood. Indeed, it was Chief Justice Sastri who had played a leading role in the *Speedy Trial* cases (1952-54), where the Court had initially struck down a statute that devised a special procedure for speedy trials in racketeering and other cases; and, later, upheld such statutes as permissible deviations from the right to equality.

Nor had the Supreme Court been rigid in its stances. It altered its views when persuaded to do so. In a remarkable *Sales Tax* case (1955), the Court had openly declared that one of its earlier decisions on sales tax was wrong – sending out the clear signal that it was both empowered and willing to change its own decisions, if necessary. Yet, what had happened was not a storm in a tea cup. The Supreme Court withstood a great deal of strong criticism. In doing so, it made an important transition to be recognised as the custodian of the Constitution, the final arbiter on constitutional interpretation and the defender of fundamental rights.

By around the middle of the 1950s, the Court's position as an institution of governance in its own right had been established. The big constitutional controversies of the day over land reform should not take one away from the vast number of other cases in which the Court had decided all kinds of matters – no less in favour of the Government. Many cases that came to the Court posed difficult questions.

In the *Religious Endowment* cases (1954), Chief Justice B.K. Mukherjea, an expert on Hindu

By around the middle of the 1950s, the Supreme Court's position as an institution of governance in its own right had been established.

The Supreme Court laid down the constitutional discipline within which transgression of fundamental rights and appeals to the public interest would be considered.

Religious Endowments, upheld the right of the State to keep an oversight over, and regulate, religious endowments from lapsing into mismanagement and corruption, while at the same time defending the rights of believers to pursue their own faith in their own way.

No less difficult were the *Cow Slaughter* cases (1958), where Chief Justice S.R. Das reconciled Muslim claims and Hindu sentiment by denying that the slaughter of cows was part of the Muslim faith, and restraining the indiscriminate killing of cows. The Court often divided on such matters – as it did in the *Ex-Communication* case (1962) where a majority of judges decided that the head of a faith had the right to ex-communicate adherents of the faith on religious grounds. The Court put restraints on the legislature and Government when they tried to impose their language policy on minority educational institutions in 1954 and again in 1962.

A very serious controversy arose in the State of Kerala where the new Communist Government of 1957 drafted a Bill to provide universal education, but imposed onerous conditions on minority educational institutions to implement this policy. There were massive protests, marches and disorder in Kerala. The President decided to refer the Bill to the Supreme Court for further scrutiny under its Advisory Jurisdiction. Chief Justice Das found a solution which prohibited excessive restraints on the minority's right to manage its own institutions, but permitted the keeping of a watchful eye to detect and deal with mismanagement.

By the beginning of the 1960s, the Supreme Court had taken a large number of controversies within its stride. Challenges to provisions of the Indian Penal Code 1860, which restricted free speech by criminalising activity that caused communal tension or affected the security of State, were upheld after reinterpreting these provisions. Pre-censorship was subjected to time and place constraints. When the freedom of the press was sought to be curtailed, by price and page restraints, in 1962 the Court protected not just free speech but the needs of the press as an institution. If there was a calm, it was because the Supreme Court had acquired a status in the minds of both the Government and the people.

The retirement of Chief Justice S.R. Das left behind a totally new Court. Chief Justice Das had been with the Court right since its inception – participating in all the controversies. Meanwhile, many new judges had been appointed; many had retired. Although there had been sharp divisions in the Court, most of these were reconciled. Once the jurisprudence of the Court was settled, those judges who had earlier taken a different view, adopted the new view as the law laid down by the Court.

As the Supreme Court advanced into the 1960s, many new differences arose. There were discernible trends in the Court. Judges like P.B. Gajendragadkar emphasised the need for social justice, to "secularise" the freedom of religion and to reconcile labour and management within the industrial disputes legislation. Judges like K. Subba Rao personified a different approach to defend civil liberties. It was Subba Rao who recognised the right to "privacy" as part of the life and liberty guaranteed by the Constitution and laid down the possibilities for a wider "due process". His judgements, too, gave rise to a new set of controversies with the Government of the day.

The old issue of the 1950s over the compensation to be paid on the acquisition of property returned to the Court. Normally, under the colonial Land Acquisition Act of 1894 the compensation paid was the market value of the property, plus a little more by way of solatium. But, new and special legislation was being enacted which deviated from market-value principles.

In the *Compensation* case (1965), Justice Subba Rao refused to accept deviations, which permitted payment of illusory sums as compensation for acquired property. But, he went further in the celebrated *Golak Nath* case in 1967 to question the powers of Parliament to amend the Constitution. By a thin majority of six to five, the Court took the view that an amending statute had no great status than any other law; and was subject to all the fundamental rights, including those which it sought to amend.

Parliament responded to this restraint on what it believed to be its sovereign power to change the Constitution in the wider interests of the nation. These controversies were to continue long after Chief Justice Subba Rao resigned to unsuccessfully contest the election for President of India.

In 1969, the ruling Congress split into the Congress (I) and the Congress (O). Mrs. Gandhi's Congress (I) remained in power and declared a programme of progressive socialism in which land would be re-distributed, banks nationalised, Privy Purses of the erstwhile princes and their families abolished and "bourgeoisie" newspapers curtailed and controlled so as to prevent them for speaking for the advantaged and business interests. The legacy of *Golak Nath* and the *Compensation* and other cases (1965) seemed to stand in the way.

Each one of the important measures undertaken by the Government did not find favour with the Supreme Court. The legislation to nationalise banks was struck down on issues of compensation in the *Bank Nationalisation* case (1970), which also took the Court's jurisprudence one important step further to create a wider due process to protect fundamental rights. The abolition of Privy Purses was upheld, with some reservation. In the *Newsprint* case (1972), the Government was not permitted to put pressure on newspapers in the matter of the supply of newsprint. Overall, the Court had not prevented the Government from doing what it wanted. But, it laid down the constitutional discipline within which transgression of fundamental rights and appeals to the public interest would be considered.

All along, the Government was uneasy with the Supreme Court's decision in *Golak Nath* (1967), which had imposed future limitations on Parliament's power to amend the Constitution. In 1971, the Twenty-fourth and Twenty-fifth Amendments to the Constitution were enacted to restore Parliament's constituent power to empower the Government to give such "amounts" of compensation as the law might permit. Some of these amendments tried to exploit possible gaps in the *Golak Nath* decision. However, a relentless attack was mounted by lawyer Nani Palkhivala on these and other amendments in the *Fundamental Rights* case (1973).

The largest ever bench of 13 judges assembled to decide whether the *Golak Nath* case was rightly decided. If the Government had hoped that the restraints on the amending power imposed by *Golak Nath* were going to be removed, it was wrong. By a majority decision, the Court went one step further than *Golak Nath*. It created a new doctrine of immense significance. It laid down that the power to amend the Constitution was subject to the limitation that the "basic structure" of the Constitution could not be taken away.

The judgement itself did not indicate what the "basic structure" of the Constitution was. It was for the Court to define the "basic structure" of the Constitution. The power of judicial review was certainly basic to the working of the Constitution. The Constitution did not permit either the legislature or the executive to determine the legality and constitutionality of their own actions. That could only be done by the judiciary. On this basis, many of the previous amendments to the Constitution, which ousted judicial scrutiny, were declared to be prospectively invalid.

The "basic structure" doctrine has become part of the constitutional discourse of the 20th century. The Supreme Court of India has limited its use to issues of fundamental import.

The wheel had turned full circle. Frequent amendments to the Constitution were looked on with disfavour. There is a nice cartoon of a bookseller refusing to sell a copy of the Constitution to a customer on the grounds that his shop did not stock periodicals! The *Fundamental Rights* case (1973) had laid down a new and exciting doctrine, reviving the view that even the sovereign power to change the Constitution was subject to limitations. The "basic structure" doctrine has become part of the constitutional discourse of the 20th century. India's Supreme Court has rightly limited its use to issues of fundamental import.

After these controversies between the Government and Parliament and the Court were brought to a rest until June 1975 when the Government declared a national Emergency, which lasted for almost two years.

III

In the year 1975, the Supreme Court completed its silver jubilee. It had been in existence for 25 eventful years. But, a few months later it had to cope with an event of monumental significance.

Around the month of June 1975, the Allahabad High Court pronounced that Mrs. Gandhi's election to Parliament in 1971 be set aside because she was guilty of a misuse of vehicles and official personnel for electoral advantage. An appeal was filed immediately in the Supreme Court where Justice Krishna Iyer delivered the judgement, granting interim protection till July when the Court reopened.

Mrs. Gandhi would continue to be a Member of Parliament, but not participate or vote in the proceedings in that capacity or draw any remuneration as a Member of the House. She could remain Prime Minister, draw the salary of Prime Minister and participate in proceedings in that capacity, but could not vote.

On the very next day – June 26, 1975 – the Government declared a national Emergency. Such an Emergency has the effect of suspending the invocation of important civil liberties and fundamental rights. During the Chinese invasion of 1962, an Emergency was declared on the grounds of "external aggression". This time, there was no external aggression. The reason given in the Proclamation was that there were "internal disturbances", which necessitated the declaration of Emergency.

Before long, in August 1975, the Emergency regime went on to make changes in the Constitution and the laws. The first set of amendments dealt with Mrs. Gandhi's election itself. Changes in the electoral law relating to the very matters on which her election was set aside immunised her election from further attack. Parliament went further to amend the Constitution itself by the Thirty-ninth Amendment, which made the election law inapplicable to the elections of the Prime Minister and Speaker of either House in respect of past and future elections. Judicial review was totally ousted.

Immediately, Shanti Bhushan, the lawyer for Mrs. Gandhi's adversary in the election, challenged the validity of the constitutional and electoral amendments. The majority of judges had little difficulty in finding the constitutional amendments violative of the rule of law and, according to one judge, fair and free election – both of which were part of the "basic structure" of the Constitution. The minority judges did not strike down the amendments, but made it clear that the amendment would not stand in the way of deciding the election to the changed electoral law, which was held to be valid. This was eminently a controversial decision, for which the Court has not escaped criticism.

But, the Emergency came at a time when Parliament was steadily moving towards the end of its five-year term. Mrs. Gandhi's government assumed near dictatorial powers. Within one year, the Forty-second Amendment was passed. It made extensive changes in the Constitution. The life of Parliament was extended beyond its five-year term. More fundamental rights were taken out of the purview of judicial scrutiny. The jurisdiction of the Courts was taken away in many different areas. Emergencies could now be declared more easily – even in parts of India. No Court could question the justification for the Emergency. Procedural requirements made it more difficult for High Courts and the Supreme Court to invalidate legislation inimical to fundamental rights. New tribunals were proposed to take over from the jurisdiction of ordinary courts.

The terms, "secularism" and "socialism", were introduced into the Preamble of the Constitution – no doubt to justify greater empowerment to the Government. Although petitions were filed before the Supreme Court to question the validity of the Forty-second Amendment, it never came to be tested in a court of law.

Meanwhile, a large number of preventive detentions were made of prominent citizens, journalists and politicians. Changes were made in the Maintenance of Internal Security Act, 1971 (MISA – as it had come to be referred to colloquially). By way of abundant caution, the Government tried to ensure that the validity of MISA and the changes in it were sought to be excluded from the purview of judicial review. This did not stop challenges being made by and on behalf of those detained.

Several High Courts in the country – Allahabad, Bombay, Delhi, Karnataka, Madhya Pradesh, Punjab and Rajasthan – rose to the challenge to hold that despite the fact that appeals could not be made to Articles 21 and 22 of the Constitution (dealing with personal liberty and preventive detention), the Courts could always examine whether the order was made by the right person, who had the power to do so, or consider whether it was made *mala fide* without due application of mind to all the relevant consideration.

When the matter reached the Supreme Court, it was heard by a Bench consisting of Chief Justice A.N. Ray and Justices H.R. Khanna, M.H. Beg, Y.V. Chandrachud and P.N. Bhagwati. All the judges, except Khanna, took the view that they did not have the power of judicial review over detentions even if the detentions were actuated by malice.

Chief Justice Ray felt that the tales of arbitrariness and woe were greatly exaggerated. Justice Beg went further to say that the "care and concern bestowed by the State authorities upon the welfare of the detenus, who are well housed, well fed and well treated, is almost maternal". Justices Bhagwati and Chandrachud accepted that judicial review was normally available in detention matters, but felt that the statute had fairly and squarely ousted the power of judicial review. Justice Khanna, the lone dissenter, thanked his colleagues for not standing in the way of his expressing his views and echoed a judicious concern:

> "More is at stake in these cases than the liberty of a few individuals or the correct construction of the wording of an order. What is at stake is the rule of law.... A dissent in a court of last resort ... is an appeal to the brooding spirit of law, to the intelligence of a future day, when a later decision may possibly correct into which the dissenting judge believes the Court to have been betrayed".

A portrait of Justice Hans Raj Khanna in Court No. 2.

In Court No. 2, where he sat as the first puisne judge, there hangs a full-length portrait of a Supreme Court judge. Presented by the Bar of the Supreme Court, it is a painting of Justice Hans Raj Khanna (left).

The Emergency came to an end in 1977. Mrs. Gandhi's Government – indeed, she herself – was defeated in the elections.

IV

Both during and after the Emergency, the Supreme Court was bitterly criticised for not defending the civil liberties of the citizens when it was called upon to do so. At first, the Court responded by issuing contempt notices to the editors of the two leading daily newspapers – the *Indian Express* and *The Times of India* for criticising the Court beyond permissible limits. Wisely, these contempt notices were withdrawn. One of the judges in the *Preventive Detention* case, former Chief Justice Ray, had retired. Justice Khanna resigned on being superseded. Chief Justice Beg had issued the contempt notices, but later withdrew them. Justice Chandrachud publicly admitted that he had made a mistake. Justice Bhagwati felt that he had been technically correct.

The Emergency was over. The Court was determined to put the Emergency behind it and start afresh.

No sooner did the new Janata Government come into power, it pre-emptively dissolved the Assemblies of nine legislatures under the Emergency power to impose President's Rule on these States. The only reason for doing so was that the new Government in power claimed that the Congress Party had been defeated so massively in the general elections to the Union Parliament that its governments in power in these nine States had forfeited their right to rule.

One kind of Emergency had replaced another. The governments of the nine affected States brought the matter to the Supreme Court, which was faced with a great dilemma once again. In the first *President's Rule* case (1977) the Court had decided that it had a limited power of judicial review, but that such an imposition of President's Rule was judicially unassailable especially after the damage was done and the Assemblies irretrievably dissolved.

Three years later, when the Congress (I) won the elections in 1980, it, too, dissolved the Assemblies of the States where the Janata Government was in power. That, too, was constitutionally permissible.

Twelve years later, in 1992, these questions arose again when the Congress Government dismissed the BJP governments in the States of Madhya Pradesh, Uttar Pradesh, Rajasthan and Himachal Pradesh after the destruction of the Babri Masjid.

Along with other impositions of President's Rule, these, too, were challenged. The Supreme Court divided – with the majority declaring varying standards of judicial review and the minority refusing to accept that review in such matters was judicially manageable. Secularism was declared to be part of the "basic structure" of the Constitution; and, therefore, a justification for imposition of President's Rule in the BJP States. The Supreme Court has yet to evolve a clear jurisprudence over the extent of its judicial review in matters relating to the declarations of Emergency.

Yet, the Court was conscious that the Emergency (1975-77) had to be declared a suspect period in the constitutional history of Indian law. When considering the *Special Courts Bill* (1979), the Supreme Court justified special treatment of political offenders during the Emergency precisely on the basis that the Emergency was as unique as it was unfortunate. Political and other offenders of that period could be treated in a class of their own. Chief Justice Chandrachud said:

> "It is unquestionably reasonable for the legislature to think that the suppression of human liberties during the period of emergency furnished an opportunity to persons holding high public or political office to commit crimes of great magnitude which were calculated to destroy democratic values".

In these and other cases, the Supreme Court enabled bringing those guilty of crimes in the Emergency to book. That this did not happen in any abundant measure is another matter.

MEASURING UP TO PEOPLE'S EXPECTATIONS

I

With the Emergency behind it, the Supreme Court entered into a new era, which is often looked at as its finest hour. It was largely due to the Court that a new public interest law was born. It is difficult to say when and how this new jurisprudence came into being. Justice Krishna Iyer received letters from Sunil Batra and Charles Sobhraj complaining about the conditions of detention in jail. People, they wrote, were shackled in chains and kept in solitary confinement for no real justification.

Without waiting for proper petitions to be drawn, the Supreme Court acted on these letters. A new epistolary jurisprudence was born. By simply writing a letter to the Chief Justice of India, or to one of the judges, a matter of public importance was heard, investigated and pronounced upon by the Court.

Once letter petitions started, there was no stopping the number of causes that would be presented to, and examined by, the Court in the public interest. The Court's procedure was democratised to establish a direct nexus with the people.

Having opened its doors to the public, the Supreme Court relaxed the rules of "standing" to allow any public-spirited citizens to bring public interest matters to it as long as they were brought bona fide by persons who had declared their identity and were not acting *benami* for some private interest. The Court promised that it did not just exist for the rich and the powerful, who could afford its processes, but for all citizens – especially, the poor, the exploited and the disadvantaged in their quest for social justice.

A large number of matters came before the Court, pertaining to under-trials languishing in jail, children who had no business to be there, women inmates of protective homes who were badly treated, bonded labour who remained virtually slaves, workers who were hopelessly exploited, the destruction of the environment, the blinding of persons in custody, custodial deaths, rapes and disappearances, ensuring land for those to whom it was promised, and so on.

In all these matters, the Supreme Court devised new methods of investigating the facts and fashioned new remedies. Since public interest letters and courses of action did not contain the complete facts, the Court appointed special commissions and committees to find out the facts and place their recommendations before it. These were then examined by all the parties, before the Court devised a remedy.

The remedies were no longer the routine remedies of declaring something invalid or passing some injunctive order. The Court ordered schematic reliefs and ensured that they were actually implemented over time – staying with the case until it was satisfied that what was required to be done was, in fact, carried out in letter and in spirit. Where people had disappeared or had been badly treated while in custody, the Court awarded them compensatory damages.

All this took place at a time when the Government was under some pressure from terrorist groups and insurgents. But the Court made it clear that whatever the compulsion, it would not allow the State to breach the plimsoll line of humanitarian rights. It was during this time that the Supreme Court ordered a settlement for the victims of the Bhopal gas tragedy in 1984, which it later revised after a public debate pointed out flaws. Public concern continues that the victims have not received their just desserts 15 years after the disaster.

II

In order to establish greater rigour in its judicial review, the post-Emergency Court expanded the concept of "reasonableness" to lay the foundations of an Indian approach to due process, made the State and public officials accountable for their arbitrariness and ensured that they kept to their promises, which were made to the people in the public interest. New doctrines of public law were devised to check the abuse of power and corruption, which were increasingly becoming a part of Indian governance.

With the Emergency behind it, the Supreme Court entered into a new era, which is often looked at as its finest hour.

Having laid down the foundations for a public interest law in the 1980s, the Supreme Court moved forward to consolidate and systematise what it had done.

But, in time, new situations developed, which found their way to the Court. In 1990, the new Janata Government decided to implement the Report of the Mandal Commission on Backward Classes (1980). The import for this implementation was that preferential job discrimination would now be extended to the Other Backward Classes (OBCs – that is other than the Backward Classes, which consisted only of the Scheduled Castes – SC – and Scheduled Tribes – ST) to the extent of 27 percent. Inevitably, caste would play an important role in determining who the OBCs were.

The Supreme Court was called upon to resolve this issue, which had erupted into a public conflagration. In the *Mandal* case (1992), while accepting "caste" as a factor for determining OBC beneficiary groups, the Court insisted that the successful creamy layers amongst the disadvantaged be eliminated from consideration and that there should be no reservations for either the Backward Classes (BC) or the OBCs in matters of promotion after five years. But, before the five years were over, Parliament amended the Constitution to permit reservations in promotional posts for the BCs alone.

Although the *Mandal* case (1992) had unravelled many of the more difficult issues, several remained. In the years to follow, the Supreme Court was called upon to examine the tensions in pursuing a policy of affirmative action in public employment and technical education and find the correct balance between the claims of equality, social justice and equal opportunity for all.

No sooner was the Mandal controversy over, a new controversy erupted over the ownership of the Babri Masjid, which various Hindu groups claimed had been built on the birthplace of Lord Rama. On December 5, 1992, Hindu miscreants, with support from the BJP in power in U.P., razed the Babri Masjid to the ground.

Following writ petitions challenging the *status quo* created by statute and a Presidential Reference to the Court to determine competing Hindu-Muslim claims to the disputed site, the Supreme Court was called upon to examine the issue. Politely declining to involve itself into historical and other questions of entitlement raised by the Presidential Reference whilst the matter was still pending, the Court approved and modified the *status quo* in a judgement that brought peace to disquiet, but did not wholly escape controversy.

Following the destruction of the Babri Masjid, the Union Government imposed Emergency President's Rule on the four BJP States of Uttar Pradesh, Madhya Pradesh, Rajasthan and Himachal Pradesh. When these impositions were considered by the Supreme Court, one of the justifications for these impositions was that they were necessary to uphold "secularism". In both the *President's Rule* case (1992) and the Babri Masjid case (1994), the Court had accepted that secularism was part of the "basic structure" of the Indian Constitution.

As it enters the new millennium, the Supreme Court can look back on what it has done with a degree of satisfaction.

These judgements are important in more than one respect. After the F*undamental Rights* case (1973), which created the "basic structure" doctrine, judicial review was declared to be part of the "basic structure" of the Constitution. So far, the "basic structure" doctrine had been used only to examine the validity of constitutional amendments. Now, the doctrine of "basic structure" was taken further. The "basic structure" of the Constitution was also identified with the "secularism" of the Constitution. Possibilities were created for taking the "basic structure" doctrine further to include democracy and, perhaps, socialism – which was also part of the amended Preamble of 1976 that had included secularism in its text.

After the *President's Rule* case (1994), the "basic structure" doctrine did not just enable challenges to constitutional amendments but also to interpret the validity of exercises of power by the legislature and executive. A new approach to the normative aspects of Indian law was slowly, but cautiously, emerging.

The creativity of the earlier public law movement was continued, but more discreetly in new areas. General norms of international law were invoked to declare new protections and procedures in cases of sexual harassment and other areas. The Court gave due recognition to "privacy" both as a constitutional concept as well as an actionable claim. In the *Criminal Due Process* cases (1997), the Court laid down new norms that had to be observed as part of the criminal due process. A priority was attached to the systematic exposition of constitutional requirements.

It was in the past few years of the 1990s that the Supreme Court was invited to consider issues concerning the environment. With almost crusading zeal, Justice Kuldip Singh and other judges heard cases to protect the Taj Mahal, India's coastline, protected forest areas, sanctuaries and parks, ground water supplies and pollution in Delhi and elsewhere in the country. New principles were evolved to deal with the environmental issues as part of an Indian and global concern.

If courts are confronted with the felt necessities of the time, the Supreme Court has to respond to issues of State lawlessness, of greed and corruption and assaults on the secular administration of the rule of law. When confronted with issues of corruption, the Court has tried to ensure that corruption does not result in guilty persons getting off the hook. New solutions have been devised and reconsidered; and will, no doubt, evolve in the future.

In the course of its history, the Supreme Court has been asked to pronounce on about half a million cases and matters. These cover many areas and disputes arising out of personal laws, civil and criminal cases, federal disputes, taxation, corporate battles against the State and each other, the rights of workers and the exploited, landlords and tenants, fundamental rights, international law and many others. This is quite an achievement for any court in the world. The Supreme Court of India has transited from being an institution of State into an institution of governance in its own right.

As it enters the new millennium, the Supreme Court can look back on what it has done with a degree of satisfaction – and a feeling that it has acquired a special place in the minds and hearts of the people of India for whom alone the Constitution exists.

President Rajendra Prasad arrives with Chief Justice S.R. Das to declare open the new Supreme Court building on August 4, 1958. Until then, the Court had fuctioned from the Chamber of Princes in the Parliament building.

From right to left: President Rajendra Prasad, Vice President S. Radhakrishnan, Chief Justice S.R. Das, Speaker of the Lok Sabha Ananthasayanam Ayyangar and Prime Minister Jawaharlal Nehru go round the Judges' Library after the Court's inauguration.

GLIMPSES OF THE SUPREME COURT BUILDING

सत्यमेवोद्धराम्यहम्

॥ यतो धर्मस्ततो जयः ॥
SUPREME COURT OF INDIA

A statue of Mahatma Gandhi graces the front lawns of the Supreme Court building.

A view of the Chief Justice's Court Room.

A full-length portrait of the fourth Chief Justice of India, Hon'ble Mr. Bijan Kumar Mukherjea, adorns the Chief Justice's Court Room.

A life-size portrait of Hon'ble Justice T.L. Venkatarama Ayyar adorns Court No. 2.

A view of Court No. 3.

CHIEF JUSTICES OF INDIA

Sir Harilal J. Kania occupies a unique place in the annals of the Indian judiciary. He was the first Indian to be appointed Chief Justice of the Federal Court of India. He was also the Court's last Chief Justice. When the Federal Court ceased to exist in 1950 and the Supreme Court of India came into being, Sir Harilal also had the distinction of being the first Chief Justice of India.

Born in Bombay on November 3, 1880, Kania had his education at Samaldas College, where he received a B.A. degree. Later, he studied at the Government Law College, where he received an LL.M. degree. Afterwards, he practised at the Bombay High Court.

In June 1930, Kania was appointed as an acting judge of the Bombay High Court. In 1931, he was made an additional judge. Two years later in 1933, he was appointed as a permanent judge of the Bombay High Court. He also twice officiated as the Court's Chief Justice.

Justice Kania was conferred with the Order of Knighthood in 1943. He died on November 6, 1951.

Justice Kania is remembered to this day for his intellect and erudition, which enabled him to become a distinguished member of the Bar and, later, the Bench, as well as for steadfastly upholding the values of honesty, truth and righteousness.

This full-length portrait of Hon'ble Sir Harilal J. Kania, the first Chief Justice of India, adorns the Chief Justice's Court Room.

Hon'ble Mr. M. Patanjali Sastri
Judge, Federal/Supreme Court (6-12-1947—6-11-1951)
Chief Justice of India (7-11-1951—3-1-1954)

Hon'ble Mr. Mehr Chand Mahajan
Judge, Federal/Supreme Court (4-10-1948—3-1-1954)
Chief Justice of India (4-1-1954—22-12-1954)

Hon'ble Mr. B.K. Mukherjea
Judge, Federal Court/Supreme Court (14-10-1948—22-12-1954)
Chief Justice of India (23-12-1954—31-1-1956)

Hon'ble Mr. S.R. Das
Judge, Federal/Supreme Court (20-1-1950—31-1-1956)
Chief Justice of India (1-2-1956—30-9-1959)

Hon'ble Mr. B.P. Sinha
Judge, Supreme Court (3-12-1954—30-9-1959)
Chief Justice of India (1-10-1959—31-1-1964)

Hon'ble Mr. P.B. Gajendragadkar
Judge, Supreme Court (17-1-1957—31-1-1964)
Chief Justice of India (1-2-1964—15-3-1966)

Hon'ble Mr. A.K. Sarkar
Judge, Supreme Court (4-3-1957—15-3-1966)
Chief Justice of India (16-3-1966—29-6-1966)

Hon'ble Mr. K. Subba Rao
Judge, Supreme Court (31-1-1958—29-6-1966)
Chief Justice of India (30-6-1966—11-4-1967)

Hon'ble Mr. K.N. Wanchoo
Judge, Supreme Court (11-8-1958—11-4-1967)
Chief Justice of India (12-4-1967—24-2-1968)

Hon'ble Mr. M. Hidayatullah
Judge, Supreme Court (1-12-1958—24-2-1968)
Chief Justice of India (25-2-1968—16-12-1970)

Hon'ble Mr. J.C. Shah
Judge, Supreme Court (12-10-1959—16-12-1970)
Chief Justice of India (17-12-1970—21-1-1971)

Hon'ble Mr. S.M. Sikri
Judge, Supreme Court (3-2-1964—21-1-1971)
Chief Justice of India (22-1-1971—25-4-1973)

Hon'ble Mr. A.N. Ray
Judge, Supreme Court (1-8-1969—25-4-1973)
Chief Justice of India (26-4-1973—28-1-1977)

Hon'ble Mr. M.H. Beg
Judge, Supreme Court (10-12-1971—28-1-1977)
Chief Justice of India (29-1-1977—21-2-1978)

Hon'ble Mr. Y.V. Chandrachud
Judge, Supreme Court (28-8-1972—21-2-1978)
Chief Justice of India (22-2-1978—11-7-1985)

Hon'ble Mr. P.N. Bhagwati
Judge, Supreme Court (17-7-1973—11-7-1985)
Chief Justice of India (12-7-1985—20-12-1986)

Hon'ble Mr. R.S. Pathak
Judge, Supreme Court (20-2-1978—20-12-1986)
Chief Justice of India (21-12-1986—18-6-1989)

Hon'ble Mr. E.S. Venkataramiah
Judge, Supreme Court (8-3-1979—18-6-1989)
Chief Justice of India (19-6-1989—17-12-1989)

Hon'ble Mr. Sabyasachi Mukherji
Judge, Supreme Court (15-3-1983—17-12-1989)
Chief Justice of India (18-12-1989—25-9-1990)

Hon'ble Mr. Ranganath Misra
Judge, Supreme Court (15-3-1983—24-9-1990)
Chief Justice of India (25-9-1990—24-11-1991)

Hon'ble Mr. K.N. Singh
Judge, Supreme Court (10-3-1986—24-11-1991)
Chief Justice of India (25-11-1991—12-12-1991)

Hon'ble Mr. M.H. Kania
Judge, Supreme Court (1-5-1987—12-12-1991)
Chief Justice of India (13-12-1991—17-11-1992)

Hon'ble Mr. L.M. Sharma
Judge, Supreme Court (5-10-1987—17-11-1992)
Chief Justice of India (18-11-1992—11-2-1993)

Hon'ble Mr. M.N. Venkatachaliah
Judge, Supreme Court (5-10-1987—11-2-1993)
Chief Justice of India (12-2-1993—24-10-1994)

Hon'ble Mr. A.M. Ahmadi
Judge, Supreme Court (14-12-1988—24-10-1994)
Chief Justice of India (25-10-1994—24-3-1997)

Hon'ble Mr. J.S. Verma
Judge, Supreme Court (3-6-1989—24-3-1997)
Chief Justice of India (25-3-1997—17-1-1998)

Hon'ble Mr. M.M. Punchhi
Judge, Supreme Court (6-10-1989—17-1-1998)
Chief Justice of India (18-1-1998—9-10-1998)

Dr. Adarsh Sein Anand, the incumbent Chief Justice of India, has had a distinguished academic and professional career.

Born at Jammu on November 1, 1936, he received his early education from Model Academy at Jammu. He graduated from Jammu and Kashmir University in 1958. He got an LL.B. degree with first class and a diploma in Labour Laws from Lucknow University in 1960. Thereafter, in 1963, he obtained a degree of Doctor of Philosophy in Laws for his dissertation "Constitutional Law of the Commonwealth" from London University.

Dr. Anand was called to the Bar from the Inner Temple, London, in 1964. He returned to India and began his practice in the Punjab & Haryana High Court at Chandigarh.

At the age of 38, Dr. Anand was appointed as an Additional Judge of the Jammu & Kashmir High Court in 1975. A few months later, he was confirmed as a permanent judge of the same court. In 1984, he was appointed as Acting Chief Justice of the Jammu & Kashmir High Court and, in less than a year, he was confirmed as the Chief Justice of the same court. In 1989, Dr. Anand was transferred as the Chief Justice of the Madras High Court. In November 1991, he was appointed as a Judge of the Supreme Court of India.

Over the years, Dr. Anand has participated in several national and international conferences. In 1996, he was unanimously elected as president of the International Institute of Human Rights Society.

Notwithstanding his busy schedule, Dr. Anand has kept his interest in academics alive. He has taught law at the Punjab University, Chandigarh; has been a member of Jammu University Council and the Faculty of Laws, Jammu University; a member of the Board of Studies, Faculty of Laws, Kashmir Univeristy; and a member of the Governing Body of Islamia College, Srinagar. He is, at present, a member of the Board of Studies, Law Faculty, Jammu University.

Dr. Anand was awarded the degree of LL.D. (Honoris Causa) by Lucknow University in 1996 and the degree of Doctor of Letters (Honoris Causa) by Jammu University in 1999. He was awarded the Fellowship of the University College, London, in 1997.

He is the author of the book titled *The Constitution of Jammu & Kashmir — Its Development & Comments.*

Dr. Anand was appointed as the Chief Justice of India on October 10, 1998.

A view of the Chief Justice's Chamber.

JUDGES OF THE SUPREME COURT

Hon'ble Sir Saiyid Fazl Ali
Judge, Federal/Supreme Court (9-6-1947—18-9-1951)

Hon'ble Mr. N. Chandrasekhara Aiyar
Judge, Supreme Court (23-9-1950—24-1-1953)

Hon'ble Mr. Vivian Bose
Judge, Supreme Court (5-3-1951—8-6-1956)

Hon'ble Mr. Ghulam Hasan
Judge, Supreme Court (8-9-1952—5-11-1954)

Hon'ble Mr. B. Jagannadhadas
Judge, Supreme Court (9-3-1953—26-7-1958)

Hon'ble Mr. P. Govinda Menon
Judge, Supreme Court (1-9-1956—16-10-1957)

Hon'ble Mr. N. H. Bhagwati
Judge, Supreme Court (8-9-1952—6-8-1959)

Hon'ble Mr. T.L. Venkatarama Ayyar
Judge, Supreme Court (4-1-1954—24-11-1958)

Hon'ble Mr. S. Jafer Imam
Judge, Supreme Court (10-1-1955—31-1-1964)

Hon'ble Mr. S.K. Das
Judge, Supreme Court (30-4-1956—28-7-1963)

Hon'ble Mr. J.L. Kapur
Judge, Supreme Court (14-1-1957—12-12-1962)

Hon'ble Mr. K.C. Das Gupta
Judge, Supreme Court (24-8-1959—2-1-1965)

Hon'ble Mr. Raghubar Dayal
Judge, Supreme Court (27-7-1960—25-10-1965)

Hon'ble Mr. N. Rajagopala Ayyangar
Judge, Supreme Court (27-7-1960—14-12-1964)

Hon'ble Mr. J.R. Mudholkar
Judge, Supreme Court (3-10-1960—3-7-1966)

Hon'ble Mr. R.S. Bachawat
Judge, Supreme Court (7-9-1964—31-7-1969)

Hon'ble Mr. V. Ramaswami
Judge, Supreme Court (4-1-1965—29-10-1969)

Hon'ble Mr. P. Satyanarayana Raju
Judge, Supreme Court (20-10-1965—20-4-1966)

Hon'ble Mr. J.M. Shelat
Judge, Supreme Court (24-2-1966—30-4-1973)

Hon'ble Mr. Vashishtha Bhargava
Judge, Supreme Court (8-8-1966—4-2-1971)

Hon'ble Mr. G.K. Mitter
Judge, Supreme Court (29-8-1966—23-9-1971)

Hon'ble Mr. C.A. Vaidialingam
Judge, Supreme Court (10-10-1966—29-6-1972)

Hon'ble Mr. K.S. Hegde
Judge, Supreme Court (17-7-1967—30-4-1973)

Hon'ble Mr. A.N. Grover
Judge, Supreme Court (12-12-1968—31-5-1973)

Hon'ble Mr. P. Jaganmohan Reddy
Judge, Supreme Court (1-8-1969—22-1-1975)

Hon'ble Mr. I.D. Dua
Judge, Supreme Court (1-8-1969—3-10-1972)

Hon'ble Mr. Subimal Chandra Roy
Judge, Supreme Court (19-7-1971—12-11-1971)

Hon'ble Mr. D.G. Palekar
Judge, Supreme Court (19-7-1971—3-9-1974)

Hon'ble Mr. H.R. Khanna
Judge, Supreme Court (22-9-1971—12-3-1977)

Hon'ble Mr. K. K. Mathew
Judge, Supreme Court (4-10-1971—2-1-1976)

Hon'ble Mr. S.N. Dwivedi
Judge, Supreme Court (14-8-1972—8-12-1974)

Hon'ble Mr. A.K. Mukherjea
Judge, Supreme Court (14-8-1972—23-10-1973)

Hon'ble Mr. A. Alagiriswami
Judge, Supreme Court (17-10-1972—16-10-1975)

Hon'ble Mr. V.R. Krishna Iyer
Judge, Supreme Court (17-7-1973—14-11-1980)

Hon'ble Mr. P.K. Goswami
Judge, Supreme Court (10-9-1973—31-12-1977)

Hon'ble Mr. R.S. Sarkaria
Judge, Supreme Court (17-9-1973—15-1-1981)

Hon'ble Mr. A.C. Gupta
Judge, Supreme Court (2-9-1974—31-12-1981)

Hon'ble Mr. N.L. Untwalia
Judge, Supreme Court (3-10-1974—31-7-1980)

Hon'ble Mr. S. Murtaza Fazl Ali
Judge, Supreme Court (2-4-1975—20-8-1985)

Hon'ble Mr. P.N. Shinghal
Judge, Supreme Court (6-11-1975—14-10-1980)

Hon'ble Mr. Jaswant Singh
Judge, Supreme Court (23-1-1976—24-1-1979)

Hon'ble Mr. P.S. Kailasam
Judge, Supreme Court (3-1-1977—11-9-1980)

Hon'ble Mr. V.D. Tulzapurkar
Judge, Supreme Court (30-9-1977—8-3-1986)

Hon'ble Mr. D.A. Desai
Judge, Supreme Court (30-9-1977—8-5-1985)

Hon'ble Mr. A.D. Koshal
Judge, Supreme Court (17-7-1978—6-3-1982)

Hon'ble Mr. O. Chinnappa Reddy
Judge, Supreme Court (17-7-1978—24-9-1987)

Hon'ble Mr. A.P. Sen
Judge, Supreme Court (17-7-1978—19-9-1988)

Hon'ble Mr. Baharul Islam
Judge, Supreme Court (4-12-1980—12-1-1983)

Hon'ble Mr. A. Varadarajan
Judge, Supreme Court (10-12-1980—16-8-1985)

Hon'ble Mr. Amarendra Nath Sen
Judge, Supreme Court (28-1-1981—30-9-1985)

Hon'ble Mr. V. Balakrishna Eradi
Judge, Supreme Court (30-1-1981—18-6-1987)

Hon'ble Mr. R.B. Misra
Judge, Supreme Court (30-1-1981—14-6-1986)

Hon'ble Mr. D.P. Madon
Judge, Supreme Court (15-3-1983—6-4-1986)

Hon'ble Mr. M.P. Thakkar
Judge, Supreme Court (15-3-1983—3-11-1988)

Hon'ble Mr. V. Khalid
Judge, Supreme Court (25-6-1984—30-6-1987)

Hon'ble Mr. G.L. Oza
Judge, Supreme Court (29-10-1985—11-12-1989)

Hon'ble Mr. B.C. Ray
Judge, Supreme Court (29-10-1985—31-10-1991)

Hon'ble Mr. M.M. Dutt
Judge, Supreme Court (10-3-1986—29-10-1989)

Hon'ble Mr. K. Jagannatha Shetty
Judge, Supreme Court (1-5-1987—14-12-1991)

Hon'ble Mr. S. Natarajan
Judge, Supreme Court (10-3-1986—28-10-1989)

Hon'ble Mr. Kuldip Singh
Judge, Supreme Court (14-12-1988—31-12-1996)

Hon'ble Mr. S. Ratnavel Pandian
Judge, Supreme Court (14-12-1988—12-3-1994)

Hon'ble Dr. T.K. Thommen
Judge, Supreme Court (14-12-1988—25-9-1993)

Hon'ble Mr. S. Ranganathan
Judge, Supreme Court (5-10-1987—30-10-1992)

Hon'ble Mr. N.D. Ojha
Judge, Supreme Court (18-1-1988—18-1-1991)

Hon'ble Mr. K. N. Saikia
Judge, Supreme Court (14-12-1988—28-2-1991)

Hon'ble Mr. V. Ramaswami
Judge, Supreme Court (6-10-1989—14-2-1994)

Hon'ble Mr. P.B. Sawant
Judge, Supreme Court (6-10-1989—29-6-1995)

Hon'ble Mr. N.M. Kasliwal
Judge, Supreme Court (6-10-1989—3-4-1993)

Hon'ble Mr. K. Ramaswamy
Judge, Supreme Court (6-10-1989—12-7-1997)

Hon'ble Ms. M. Fathima Beevi
Judge, Supreme Court (6-10-1989—29-4-1992)

Hon'ble Mr. K. Jayachandra Reddy
Judge, Supreme Court (11-1-1990—14-7-1994)

Hon'ble Mr. S.C. Agrawal
Judge, Supreme Court (11-1-1990—4-9-1998)

Hon'ble Mr. R.M. Sahai
Judge, Supreme Court (11-1-1990—24-6-1995)

Hon'ble Mr. Yogeshwar Dayal
Judge, Supreme Court (22-3-1991—2-8-1994)

Hon'ble Mr. S. Mohan
Judge, Supreme Court (7-10-1991—10-2-1995)

Hon'ble Mr. B.P. Jeevan Reddy
Judge, Supreme Court (7-10-1991—13-3-1997)

Hon'ble Mr. G.N. Ray
Judge, Supreme Court (7-10-1991—30-4-1998)

Hon'ble Mr. R.C. Patnaik
Judge, Supreme Court (3-12-1991— 30-5-1992)

Hon'ble Mr. N.P. Singh
Judge, Supreme Court (15-6-1992—24-12-1996)

Hon'ble Mr. S.P. Bharucha
Judge, Supreme Court (1-7-1992—till date)

Hon'ble Mr. N. Venkatachala
Judge, Supreme Court (1-7-1992—2-7-1995)

Hon'ble Mr. M.K. Mukherjee
Judge, Supreme Court (14-12-1993— 30-11-1998)

Hon'ble Mr. Faizan Uddin
Judge, Supreme Court (14-12-1993—4-2-1997)

Hon'ble Mr. B.L. Hansaria
Judge, Supreme Court (14-12-1993—24-12-1996)

Hon'ble Mr. S.C. Sen
Judge, Supreme Court (11-6-1994—20-12-1997)

Hon'ble Mr. K.S. Paripoornan
Judge, Supreme Court (11-6-1994—11-6-1997)

Hon'ble Mr. S.B. Majmudar
Judge, Supreme Court (19-9-1994—till date)

Hon'ble Ms. Sujata V. Manohar
Judge, Supreme Court (8-11-1994—27-8-1999)

Hon'ble Mr. G.T. Nanavati
Judge, Supreme Court (6-3-1995—till date)

Hon'ble Mr. S. Saghir Ahmad
Judge, Supreme Court (6-3-1995—till date)

Hon'ble Mr. K. Venkataswami
Judge, Supreme Court (6-3-1995—18-9-1999)

Hon'ble Mr. B.N. Kirpal
Judge, Supreme Court (11-9-1995—till date)

Hon'ble Mr. G.B. Pattanaik
Judge, Supreme Court (11-9-1995—till date)

Hon'ble Mr. S.P. Kurdukar
Judge, Supreme Court (29-3-1996—15-1-2000)

Hon'ble Mr. K.T. Thomas
Judge, Supreme Court (29-3-1996—till date)

Hon'ble Mr. M. Jagannadha Rao
Judge, Supreme Court (21-3-1997—till date)

Hon'ble Mr. V.N. Khare
Judge, Supreme Court (21-3-1997—till date)

Hon'ble Mr. D.P. Wadhwa
Judge, Supreme Court (21-3-1997—till date)

Hon'ble Mr. M. Srinivasan
Judge, Supreme Court (25-9-1997—till date)

Hon'ble Mr. S. Rajendra Babu
Judge, Supreme Court (25-9-1997—till date)

Hon'ble Mr. Ajay Prakash Misra
Judge, Supreme Court (4-12-1997—till date)

Hon'ble Mr. S.S.M. Quadri
Judge, Supreme Court (4-12-1997—till date)

Hon'ble Mr. M.B. Shah
Judge, Supreme Court (9-12-1998—till date)

Hon'ble Mr. D.P. Mohapatra
Judge, Supreme Court (9-12-1998—till date)

Hon'ble Mr. U.C. Banerjee
Judge, Supreme Court (9-12-1998—till date)

Hon'ble Mr. R.C. Lahoti
Judge, Supreme Court (9-12-1998—till date)

Hon'ble Mr. N. Santosh Hegde
Judge, Supreme Court (8-1-1999—till date)

Hon'ble Mr. R.P. Sethi
Judge, Supreme Court (8-1-1999—till date)

Hon'ble Mr. S.N. Phukan
Judge, Supreme Court (28-1-1999—till date)

Hon'ble Ms. Ruma Pal
Judge, Supreme Court (28-1-2000—till date)

Hon'ble Mr. Doraiswamy Raju
Judge, Supreme Court (28-1-2000—till date)

Hon'ble Mr. Yogesh Kumar Sabharwal
Judge, Supreme Court (28-1-2000—till date)

ATTORNEY GENERAL FOR INDIA

The Attorney General for India holds office under Article 76 of the Constitution. He is appointed by the President of India and must be a person eligible to be appointed as a judge of the Supreme Court of India. As the principal law officer of the Government, he acts as its lead counsel in the Supreme Court and has the duty to give advice to the Union of India. Besides his work for the Government, as observed by the Court, he "in some respects, acts as the friend, philosopher and guide of the Court".

Under the Constitution, the Attorney General has the right to speak, and otherwise to take part, in the proceedings of either House, any joint sitting of the two Houses, and any Committee of Parliament of which he may be named a member. He, however, is not entitled to vote.

Over the past 50 years, the following distinguished lawyers have held the office of Attorney General for India.

M.C. Setalvad (26-1-1950—31-12-1962)

C.K. Daphtary (2-3-1963—30-10-1968)

Niren De (1-11-1968—31-3-1977)

S.V. Gupte (1-4-1977—8-8-1979)

Lal Narayan Sinha (9-8-1979—8-8-1983)

K. Parasaran (9-8-1983—8-12-1989)

Soli J. Sorabjee (8-12-1989—2-12-1990)

G. Ramaswamy (2-12-1990—9-11-1992)

Milon K. Banerji (24-11-1992—8-7-1996)

Ashok H. Desai (9-7-1996—6-4-1998)

Soli J. Sorabjee (7-4-1998—till date)

M.C. Setalvad

Soli J. Sorabjee

SOLICITOR GENERAL OF INDIA

In addition to the Attorney General for India, there is also the Solicitor General of India. As of now, the following distinguished lawyers have held the office of Solicitor General of India.

C.K. Daphtary (1951—1-3-1963)

H.N. Sanyal (2-3-1963—9-9-1964)

S.V. Gupte (16-9-1964—16-9-1967)

Niren De (30-9-1967—30-10-1968)

Jagdish Swarup (5-6-1969—4-6-1972)

L.N. Sinha (17-7-1972—5-4-1977)

S.N. Kaicker (5-4-1977—2-8-1979)

Soli J. Sorabjee (9-8-1979—25-1-1980)

K. Parasaran (6-3-1980—8-8-1983)

Milon K. Banerji (4-4-1986—3-4-1989)

Ashok H. Desai (18-12-1989—2-12-1990)

A.D. Giri (4-12-1990—1-12-1991)

Dipankar P. Gupta (9-4-1992—5-8-1996)

T.R. Andhyarujina (6-8-1996—22-4-1998)

N. Santosh Hegde (23-4-1998—7-1-1999)

Harish N. Salve (4-11-1999—till date)

The highest administrative officer of the Supreme Court of India is the Registrar General. However, until 1987, the Ragistrar was the highest officer. Over the years, these posts have been held by:

REGISTRAR

P.N. Murthy (26-1-1950—4-1-1956)

K. Krishnaswami Aiyer (5-1-1956—1-4-1956)

Arindam Dutt (2-4-1956—14-6-1962)

S.N. Sharma (1-7-1962—15-3-1964)

Y.D. Desai (13-8-1963—19-4-1969)

C.V. Rane (9-6-1969—19-10-1971)

M.P. Saxena (20-10-1971—30-4-1979)

S.K. Gupta (16-7-1973—1-1-1978)

R. Narasimhan (16-1-1978—31-3-1984)

R. Subba Rao (1-5-1979—31-3-1986)

A.N. Oberai (1-4-1986—29-2-1988)

REGISTRAR GENERAL

Sankatha Rai (1-6-1987—3-11-1992)

M.S.A. Siddiqui (9-11-1992—26-9-1994)

Chandresh Bhushan (27-9-1994—27-4-1998)

Bhanwar Singh (27-4-1998—26-3-1999)

Lal Chand Bhadoo (27-3-1999—till date)

A view of the Judges' Library.

PREAMBLE TODAY

WE, THE PEOPLE OF INDIA, having solemnly resolved to constitute India into a SOVEREIGN SOCIALIST SECULAR DEMOCRATIC REPUBLIC and to secure to all its citizens:

JUSTICE, social, economic and political;

LIBERTY of thought, expression, belief, faith and worship;

EQUALITY of status and of opportunity;
and to promote among them all

FRATERNITY assuring the dignity of the individual and the unity and integrity of the Nation;

IN OUR CONSTITUENT ASSEMBLY this twenty-sixth day of November, 1949, do HEREBY ADOPT, ENACT AND GIVE TO OURSELVES THIS CONSTITUTION.

SUPREME COURT OF INDIA

